ON THE SUBJECT OF ENLIGHTENMENT

Boots on the Ground

AUDREY WEIGEL

Copyright © 2024

This book is not meant to be used, nor should it be used, to diagnose or treat any medical or psychological condition. Readers are advised to consult their own medical advisors whose responsibility it is to determine the condition of, and best treatment for, the reader.

Cover design by Audrey Weigel
photos Bryce Canyon 2007

Editor
Charlotte Sellers

Published by Stellar, Inc.

Hardcover ISBN: 978-1-7360270-4-2
Paperback ISBN 978-1-7360270-3-5
Kindle ISBN: 978-1-7360270-6-6

All rights are reserved. There is to be no reproduction of this book, in part or whole. 'Fair use' reproduction is allowed, i.e., as quotations in articles or reviews – without prior written permission of the author.

Author can be reached at stellarbyaudrey@gmail.com
Comments and inquiries welcome.

TABLE OF CONTENTS

1. INTRODUCTION v
2. AWAKENING EXPERIENCE 1
3. FULL AWARENESS TRAJECTORY 6
4. CLEARING AND KEEPING CLEAR 9
5. THE EVERYDAY LIFE OF A SEEKER 12
6. IT AN INSIDE JOB 15
7. LIVING ABUNDANTLY 18
8. THE ULTIMATE GIFT – LOVE 22
9. DISCOVERING YOUR TRUE NATURE 25
10. SPIRIT PULLS YOU ASIDE TO REVEAL DIAMONDS 28
11. TO BE HELD IN THE BOSOM OF ETERNITY 33
12. HEART POWER 36
13. THERE IS NO DEATH, ONLY NEW BEGINNINGS 40
14. PURE PRESENCE 43
15. LIVING IN FLOW 47
16. LOVE WRIT LARGE 50
17. INTEGRATED PEACE 54
18. SERENDIPITOUS SURRENDER 57
19. VICTIMHOOD VS FREEDOM 60
20. EXUDING PRESENCE 64
21. LIVING LOVE 69
22. NON-ATTACHMENT 72
23. EMBODY WHAT YOU LEARN 76

24.	THE IMPLICATIONS OF AWAKENING	80
25.	VULNERABILITY IN POWER	83
26.	THE ETHER OF YOUR BEING	88
27.	THE MOTIONLESS MOTION	91
28.	TO MY GRANDSON	95
29.	PASSION	99
30.	BEING	103
31.	A NEW WAY OF BEING	105

INTRODUCTION

Two and a half years ago, I was given the opportunity to write an article in a national magazine, VEDIC ASTROLOGY, that was just starting up. Vedic Astrology is an ancient astrology that came out of India. My articles are about being in your true nature, an awakened or enlightened state. I draw from my knowledge and journey in this subject. These chapters are the articles that I have written for this magazine each month.

I come from a middle class tried and true American family. Always curious about the deeper questions of life, I then took on studying them and applying what I learned throughout my life.

In my first book, ALTERED PERCEPTION TO FULL AWARENESS, I describe my Enlightenment experience and how it impacted my life for the next approximately ten years.

I decided to write this present book with the 30 magazine articles because I felt it rich in both insight and application of those interested in living an enlightened life.

Each month I wrote the articles, I would take the topic that I had learned during that period last month and write an article. Every morning, I do one and a half hours of spiritual study and then I go about incorporating that into my life, actually living that principle or way of being. Over this two-and-a-half-year period I have made considerable progress and rest in my being to a satisfying peaceful degree of immersion.

If you are reading this book, then I know you are a seeker, and I celebrate that. My hope is that you can relate to some part of what I present, and it clarifies things a little further so that you have more insight and courage to proceed on to the next step in your journey.

AWAKENING EXPERIENCE

My background in being a seeker started early. Being a curious child did get me in trouble, once for walking home from school along the railroad tracks and another occasion of entering the opposite sex restroom. At age 10, I replied, when I grow up I want to be a wise old woman. This due to being ever puzzled by the older people about me, they just didn't make sense to me and I was going to figure it out. From age 15 on, I was a seeker of the answers to the big questions in life. Ever on the move with those, I became a nurse to experience birth, death and everything in between. Attending both psychotherapy and healing schools throughout my adulthood. I had attended different protestant religions during my childhood and then joined a wonderful family-oriented religion as an adult.

My goal as a middle-aged adult was Christ consciousness. I have since moved on to being spiritual with no specific religion.

A couple weeks before my awakening experience, I remember stepping out of my off-grid cabin and feeling quite empty inside myself. I thought, that's curious that after all my healing work I came to being empty inside, clear, no real person present. On reflection, I see that that was necessary to clear enough space to have clear sight for what I was about to experience.

I bred german shepherds and was taking my dogs for a walk on my 20 acres, as was often my practice, in the late afternoon. I looked up at the far mountains and my perception of the whole scene changed. I became the scene; I was more present than I had ever been. I was also the atmosphere, felt I was a speck of me in and of the entire scene, only my consciousness, an astute observer and nevertheless a part of the atmosphere that was teeming with power and love. I was incredulous and rendered me dumbfounded, I panicked and thought I might be dead, as I had no feeling in my body, only this me that was delightfully present and apart of everything. I thumped my chest, I sigh of relief that I still had a body, not dead. Then my attention went back to the experience, I felt like an acute observer and thought to myself that that made sense because in real life I was quite the curious observer. It was marvelous, the level of presence and aliveness I felt, I thought it similar to being a child acute presence. I knew it was real, more than regular life afforded, spoke to its own authenticity. I had had many spiritual experiences, of course none of this magnitude or character, and knew to ask a question. There was no one to ask it too, except that marvelous atmosphere/seemed real enough to be a presence. So, I asked a distant point between myself and the hills, in that direction there were hills. Do you have anything to tell me? The answer came clear and with more love that I had ever experienced here on Earth, I heard 'I have been with you every moment of your life.' My heart swelled and I teared up, speechless. I was so touched because I had suffered so much in my life and felt alone. To know that I was not alone and someone or some force loved me that much was overwhelming. I was saturated in the acuteness of my presence, this new experience of being and the love that I never knew existed. I came back to a state of true astonishment. Walked back to my cabin and went up to the bedroom, for some reason. Then I went back into it. Again, feeling acute presence and no body sensations. I felt like a pair of detached huge eyeballs, like one of those pictures of a frog sitting there with their huge eyes showing and all you see is eyes. I look around and all objects are glowing, even the file cabinet. It was all sacred. I enjoyed the incredulousness and the sacredness. Just a plain old bedroom, I was able to see it in a wonderful new way.

Well, what does one do for the evening after all that? I was truly self- absorbed. I knew I had an awakening experience; some call it an enlightenment experience. However, my intuition said that I needed to still get to embodying it in my regular life. I read up on it online and concluded that I had had the usual/unusual awakening experience. Why me? Best I can come to this answer is that all my healing work and my unrelenting intent was helpful.

That evening, I ordered books that seemed to relate and that might help me because now I was driven to understand and return. I wanted to live that and stay there. It was a thirst that was so unreasonable but needed to be satisfied.

One of the books I ordered was of an American that had studied Buddhism and had the same experience as I, the awakening experience. He said it would take 7 – 9 years to assimilate this and live it. I thought, my gosh I have done decades of healing work and it will take me 5 years. How wrong I was, It has taken me 10 years to abide in that state, my true unfathomable immense unlimited no self self.

Why so long you ask? Memories needed to be erased and a system of how to deal with them when they arose needed to be developed. Yes, this was done on a day-to-day basis throughout those ten years. I would have a new question every day, study it out through reading and contemplation, come to a theory, try the theory out in my life and then keep what I found worked, what was true in my then found experience of that subject. My questions were both spiritual and secular, although as you see with the following question, it started off secular and turned in to both. For instance, I was faced with a financial crisis and common solutions but came to an uncommon understanding. The question that arose was, what was the way I could support myself that was true to who I was and where I was at at the time? I had been a psych nurse for 15 years and had been laid off two years previous, due to the economy, and worked part time online for my daughter at the time. My dilemma was whether I should go back to nursing and not have any financial worries. I tried it out, went on many interviews but going back to being a nurse did not feel right, through all those interviews. I could have pressed on, but it felt like I just needed to stay home and draw my line in the sand for that, for my truth. I got brave and did that and kept up my daily spiritual studies, tending to my off grid living quarters, attending to new puppy litters, and living a mostly quiet contemplative life. This served me well and financially did work out.

Through this lifestyle and a move to a condo in the city, I worked through the stages that I needed to go through in order to embody, allow sprit to awaken that inner being of self-knowledge and connectedness that is the foundation of my happiness now.

At present, I write, sew, paint for my creative engagements. I live in my own residence in a small town with my husband and son with frequent activities with my other children and their families. Life is always presenting me with new challenges but now I have the peaceful wonderful perspective to meet them all with. Thank you for listening to a segment of my journey. I trust it served you.

FULL AWARENESS TRAJECTORY

There are stages of evolvement in becoming fully aware. Gradually, as the air becomes clearer one can see clearer. It is necessary to clear misconceptions that we have acquired along the way. Any problem or conflict involves a misconception(s). That gives fertile ground to work with in this modern life.

As with any endeavor, there must be intent. A person will be tested beyond their limits and must stretch to go on. They must be willing to give up anything in their life that is required. The first book I read, after my awareness experience, was 'The End of Your World' by Adyashanti. He is an American that followed the Buddhist path. I had to smile at the title because that was so succinctly appropriate.

I was intent in wanting to know the answers to the big questions in life, no matter what it took. I followed the American deep healing path, psychotherapy, Gestalt, hypnotherapy, Rapid Eye, and Monroe Institute. I gradually cleared aware many false concepts that ran my life. Any method will work, if you are clearing away misconceptions and seeing the results in a freer more authentic life. It has to do with the disposition of the person, as to what path works effectively for them. All roads lead to Rome, as the saying goes.

Then one day, 40 years later into my adulthood, I was given a powerful awareness experience, like the famous ones you hear about. Unmistakably of another reality, than known earth life. Showing me that I am not what I thought I was, pure being with no identity and no history. Not of this body. Being permeated by power and love, through and through, I was that. Affirmed for my preciousness, much more than I had ever experienced. This was like opening the front door to my house and being blinded by the light, so much so that it startled me and rendered me short of breath.

I intuitively knew I was not fully awakened unless I could embody what I had experienced in my everyday life. I used the deep healing techniques, I had been schooled in, to clear away more misconceptions that arose. I also started dipping into Eastern teachings. For seven years, through a daily practice of morning study, inquiring, finding answers and application in my daily life, I was able to embody this awareness. I became the awareness and thereby fully aware.

However, this full awareness was not stable, and I could be thrown off the horse. Through invading thoughts or circumstances, both the same, I would go back into semi regular states of consciousness, limited.

Through the next three years I practiced being able to control my mind. This came through learning to refocus when thoughts came up and an acceptance of my sacredness. So even though I knew the truth, there was still the invading of old thinking and circumstances and further need of learning. I would call that the remnants of clearing and choosing the truth at any given moment.

Now I live being fully present. Happiness is inherent in being fully present. There are conundrums that do come up but they are solved quickly.

I never imagined that being fully aware, present, and being intimately a part of everything is the same, to the point where there is no distinction between the two. I now know that to be true.

CLEARING AND KEEPING CLEAR

Focusing on what I would call the second most important step in the awakening process, decluttering. The first being, INTENT. Whether you are leading up to the awakening experience or processing it into your life, decluttering is crucial. Other words used synonymously for decluttering are clearing, healing, aligning, resolving. It's all those misconceptions and negative experiences that we buy in to as we go along in life and then frame our lives around them.

To give a more practical application of that I outline my journey with decluttering. I first started out, with a mostly normal but dysfunctional type upbringing. Per normal sequencing, I reached adulthood scathed. I found I was lacking in my ability to cope with adult life in my relationships. I went to psychotherapy for 20 years on and off. I trained as a facilitator in a Gestalt healing group and processed through more. I went through Hypnotherapy School but never certified. Attended workshops at Rapid Eye Institute and Monroe Institute. Traveled to Peru and took Ayahuasca with a native medicine man. My aim was to heal my dysfunctions so I would not pass it on to my children and Christ consciousness.

Then I had my Awakening experience in 2012. I took to Eastern religions after my Awakening Experience. I learned that I had an authentic Awakening experience. Then my goal became to embody my awakening experience and live it in daily life. After that it was the same decluttering because fears and misconceptions resurfaced on a deeper level. Daily spiritual studies, inquiry, and the application of what I further learned in my daily life was instrumental.

My decluttering was through deep subconscious healing techniques and experiences. This is how I learn best. These methods are frightening to most people because it gets down to brass tacks and resolves the inner conflicts quickly. However, it worked for me. Different people have different dispositions. There is a plethora of methods to choose from, traditional religion, meditation, yoga, traditional & alternative psychotherapy, astrology, are just a few.

Through all this, my intent was fully committed. It did not matter whether it was attainable by normal standards. It was what I was motivated to attain.

The reward was living more fully every day, as I learned more and had the ability to be more. Even though it is a deconstruction project, it feels like you are attaining more, I would say it was reclaiming more of myself. I believe that this looking within and decluttering/reclaiming is the most difficult thing to do in life.

Is an awakening experience necessary? I would say yes because it shows you what you really are and what you are indelibly apart of. Sri Nisargadatta, an Indian sage, called it 'a vision of the universe'. In our regular lives, we have no clue about this except to touch on snippets of it, which is what motivates us in wanting more or shall we say, the whole enchilada. An awakening experience cannot be order up. It comes of its own biding. But you can do things to prepare yourself and I would say put it within your realm of possibilities.

Decluttering is important because it is the bridge to an Awakening experience and the bridge after to embodying it and living an awakened life. It is a practical system to clear unnecessary erroneous thinking. Then with an awakening experience you see your true universal nature. What is left is you, pure and simple, on the same wavelength as God/universe. The benefit is that you will lead a singular/universal life of peace, magic, and plenty, no matter what your circumstances.

Ramana Maharshi, well known Indian guru, said that what it is, to be more accurate, is you and the universe/God are the same reality. Literally, not different. I think of it as if I were driving in an invisible car. We'd both be going the same speed and I would not know that I was even in a car. Same wavelength, traveling at the same speed.

THE EVERYDAY LIFE OF A SEEKER

A seeker is one that knows there is more to this life than what is presented, or they have experienced snippets of what they want to follow because it is so delicious. Sometimes the journey is invoked from a traumatic experience where they have tasted these things and sometimes from a deeply positive experience where they have experienced the spiritual realm. They are now willing to put the time and effort into this pursuit. It has been so moving that their whole life is oriented to this end now.

It is helpful to see the different stages of the seeker, to an awakened life. This can be found in Zen depicted in the The Ten Oxherding Pictures. Type in the Google search bar: The Ten Oxherding Pictures–Tricycle: The Buddhist Review. Then select the website: https//tricycle.org Magazine If you do not have a computer, this can be found in any library. You may wonder how this can be done while living an ordinary life, not monastic. It is a unique way of living but it is doable.

Priority, you are a seeker. It is like this overwhelming urge that takes precedence over all other. It is your central aim in life. You do not get to vote about it. It just is. It is necessary that it is this paramount because it will require everything that you have, willingly on your part but nevertheless arduous.

The commitment is there. Now you need a place where you can be taught. Taught how to bridge the gap between common life and a spiritual life, to begin with. Throughout my life, a common life, I have employed many helpful places to learn, religion, psychology, healing work, daily study, and workshops. There is a plethora available. The main point was that I was always engaged in a practice, no matter what was going on in my life. The practice varied according to what served me at that stage.

How that worked: I went through my regular life and had questions. Like simple things that come up, how do I talk with people when I am a seeker and there are no common interests? I felt I had to go to their topics and spout my knowledge of that and engage that topic. It was a puzzle to me. I brought that to my morning study. I read many ideas on the topic from my valued teachers. I decided on one new approach that made the most sense to me. That you cannot compromise your own space and can listen to what is important to them, while not actively engaging in the topic that they brought up. I tried it out in my daily life, and it worked like a charm. I could retain my energy introspective level while still maintaining a relationship. Not only that, but it served the other person better because they were being heard. ThisT was fortunate to come upon a solution. Not always did it come so readily, many times I would study, postulate a resolution, and not have it work so well. Which required more study and repeating the process. Then there is the circumstance that nothing works, being true to yourself and others, and you must walk away.

When I raised children, I employed the formula: teach, support, make accountable. For instance, I would teach a chore, do it with them and then make them accountable for it. They did not get paid for that chore unless it was 95% done right. If they did not want to do the chore, then it was offered to others. This is where they earned their independent spending money.

Teach, support, and make accountable applied to my spiritual learning. I put myself in a system, morning study, whereby I could be taught. I supported myself by going to teachers and friends. I made myself accountable by trying out the solutions and staying at the drawing board until I found a solution.

I know I am talking of mundane applications but that is where the spiritual community has it wrong in thinking that spirituality is far removed from daily life. There's an old saying, you cannot get to nirvana except by samsara. What this means is, you have a lot of work to do through samsara, your everyday mind set, to get to nirvana, an awakened life. Rarely does one get there in one fell swoop. It takes time and effort to work through all the misconceptions and excessive drives, to gradually learn and open to a new life.

There are times of great leaps of insight but then it is followed by periods of catch up, where you reconcile, one by one dispose of your old positions that had been holding you back.

It is a journey of a lifetime to enrich our lives more and more. The awakened life is not some fluff in the sky, but something that you come to understand through experience by and by and then live by and by until it absorbs you and there is no distinction between life and yourself.

IT AN INSIDE JOB

Age 20, my class instructor asked, how can you change the world? I answered, the changes must come from within. You've heard the saying, that we are our own worst enemies. The origin and solution can be found by looking in the mirror. Sometimes this entails taking external action but often not, it is an internal shift.

Folks think problems exist in the outside world. This is a form of denial. The stimulus might be external, but we are the final authority. When we take responsibility in our personal lives and have the courage to look within, we can open ourselves up to whole new areas that we henceforth have cut ourselves off from. Is this easy, I would postulate that this is the hardest thing you will ever do. Face your fears, after all this is what you have been avoiding. Most of my adult life has been riddled with fears and anxiety, which continually showed up in my outer life and I had to deal with them or remain in that state. I found that in each instance that I had made up stuff that was simply not true. I took my problems to friends, counselors, the microscope of spiritual study, trying out new methods in my life, whatever it took.

Let's look at the overall picture. The self seeks its' source, its true nature. Anything that stands in its way, will show up as conflicts and problems. Conflicts and problems are not part of your true nature. They are real to the human experience but not part of our true nature. Through no fault of our own, we buy in to these untruths that we are taught or make up ourselves, from a negative experience, i.e. I am unworthy. This is done to survive, emotionally, physically, or intellectually. Then they come back to bite us because they are not part of our true nature. These untruths are seen, by us, as necessary to survive, i.e. I must give others what they want to get what I need. We get it all mixed up and then think we need it to survive, hence our fear and anxiety. But it is just not so. We need motivation and courage to approach all that and uncover the truth.

Where can we do this work? Everyday. The wise person learns from everything. It is hard to look at where we might have contributed negatively to a situation. The question can be asked, what fear did I act on? That's where the little known within us surfaces. A more conscious approach involves taking action to heal, i.e. meditation group, reiki, gestalt, hypnotherapy, healing focused workshops, astrology reading, yoga group. Your struggles will surface during these sessions and there will be support there to assist. Support is important, these things that surface are sometimes distressing, hence they have been avoided for so long.

When you know there has been movement, you find yourself acting differently in the same circumstance that was in question, i.e. you are at a party and find you are not boastful but more receptive.

We are our true nature at any given moment. However, there are so many layers that we have heaped on, through no fault of our own, that we cannot feel or enjoy ourselves at a deep real interactive level with what is important to us.

There is no judgement, what is important to one person is not important to another.

It is not a head trip where you learn and mimic the qualities of being in your true nature. It is real and right now, and you feel it coursing through you. This is a natural process; it is arrived at by dismantling/realizing the untruths that you operate under and piece by piece embracing new parts of your true nature. It takes courage to embrace those newly discovered parts, although they have been there all along. They seem foreign at first, but their truth is irrefutable.

Does awakening play a part in all this? We are talking an awakening experience. Yes, but it is a huge realization along the way. Totally foreign to anything you have known previously, although glorious and incomparable in its value. It is not an achievement and must be incorporated, embodied. This will come up against fears and anxieties from past programming and once again, must be worked through in the method that works best for you.

There is this place, that is where you are comfortable, at home, at peace and yet it is all your dreams come true because you are deeply involved, so much so that you seem to flow right along and enjoy yourself, you do not think it over. There is a whole new world inside you and outside that is inextricably connected.

LIVING ABUNDANTLY

As you become more and more aware, you will become more and more the essence of you that inherently vibrates with life. This inner life is in perfect synchronicity with the outer. It resonates and vibrates along with the whole. That's why it is said that you become the whole. You don't disappear in the whole, but you are in synchronicity with the whole. Is a matter of fact, that is when your true gifts are discovered and can serve the whole by being so integrated that your true gifts stand out.

In relationship, there is no relationship, relating. Because you are in such synchronicity with another that you are aware of their true nature, through being aware of yours, it is a communion between their being and yours. This happens whether they agree or not. It is your knowledge of their presence.

I am talking about living from an awakened self. We are not talking about living higher laws. It is actually boots on the ground, everyday living. You will be 100 % invested, body, mind, and heart. It is not a head trip but like the moment before death and you are fully invested, present.

This all comes along with its own eco-system. All the adjectives that are associated with being an awakened person are the result of this eco-system. In this, there is different internal processing, involving stability and positivity. The external world of everyday life is present but does not register like it did before awakening. You are still a part of it, but you see it for what it is. You also see events and communications for what they are, mostly conjecture and drama from wounding. Empathy abounds. You appreciate the wonders of life, simple things resonate in waves. Sad things touch your heart and motivate you to serve with your gifts.

From your perspective, rarely can anyone recognize and relate to your true nature. Only you know that. You are happy in this aloneness and treasure it, it has rewards of its own. A clue, it is like what you were in your younger years, and you were fully satisfied with going about your activities. There's real joy in that. Now you inherently don't buy in to the negativity, as well. Now when someone tries to use or abuse you, you recognize it as something foreign to your true nature. You now vibrate with life.

Am I talking pie in the sky? No, this is not a fairy tale but within the reach of every human on this Earth. We are here to have our own experiences and work out our own return to our true nature, that basic place where you know you are home. We are here to be alone, have our own experiences, make our own decisions, revise our plans, and find things we previously did not know, but seem strangely familiar.

I have never made significant steps in this process of return to my true nature without support and love from others. They did not need to be close relationships, just to be there at the right junctures in my process. I for one have been easily frightened and have been prone to flights of the imagination that took me on days, weeks, years of stress. I do have an excess of courage born of the knowledge that the only way to get through something is to hold my breath and go. It takes a lot of courage to see that your former ways do not work and that you must walk in to the unknown and try that out. I needed support and love and I was given what I needed to transition at each juncture. I encourage you to find this at times of bewilderment, better yet, ongoing throughout your process.

Now we will talk practically. In this growth/return to true nature process, it is basically a deconstruction of all the false beliefs we hold, i.e., you are far different than I am. To make something happen you need a vision and then a means to bring that about. There are many healing/awareness processing systems. Basically, left brain, right brain and in between. Left-brain would be concentration or Karma yoga. Right brain would be meditation or Bhakti yoga. In the middle would be contemplation or Advaita Vedanta. Each individual has a propensity for one of these three general types of healing paths. Modern healing systems or ancient spiritual systems will generally fall in to one of these three broad categories. I ascribe to the path of contemplation and do not believe anything that I have not experienced, either externally or internally. You need some sort of system to work your vision of awakening through, some structure, as humans are setup today.

That there is more to life than you presently know, starts out as a flicker. Then as you slowly incorporate that in your life, more opens and you muster the courage to walk through that door and in to that unknown, and so it repeats itself. This is over the course of many years. You have cleared away more and more and your life becomes richer and richer. Your capacity to process conundrums increases exponentially. Until finally the door to your true nature is flung open and all on the outside is in synchronicity with the inside. Then you are living from the joy in your heart and life teems all around you and within.

"If the doors of perception were cleansed every thing would appear to man as it is, Infinite. For man has closed himself up, till he sees all things thro' narrow chinks of his cavern."
By William Blake

THE ULTIMATE GIFT – LOVE

The bane of my life has been relationships. Six marriages, I hope I have learned a thing or two. But I want to approach this from an individual awakened perspective.

The bedrock of relationships can be found in the individuals that make up those interactions. How conscious are the participants? This will determine each participants stability and the quality of their contribution. If more on the unconscious side, then it will manifest in being overly sensitive and acting out, whilst blaming the other. If more conscious, then behaviors can be processed and the other can be seen more clearly, while caring for our partner. An awakened relationship would be for each to have their own separate happiness, be honest and contribute to the other. At that point, you are self-generating your own happiness and communing with another is a most delicious. It is interesting that this does not have to be reciprocated. Just viewing another's higher self can be bonified elating.

I am going to take liberty here in relating a story from my own life. When I was in my 40s I needed a healthy relationship, by modern psychology terms, and I divorced due to not getting this. Notice the blame I put on the other person, while my behaviors were not stellar. But in my 60s, the person I was in love with had PTSD and could not deliver a healthy relationship. I was committed to this person. I will not lie; it was distressing at times. However, I had learned how to respectfully and kindly communicate how I felt, why I felt that way and what I wanted, through years of therapy. This situation did not influence my level of happiness. I was living an awakened life. My happiness was self-generated every day. He was conscious enough that he saw his behavior as undesirable and counterproductive and changed his ways, through deep introspection. I recently had a conversation with him. I wanted to know how all this played out in his mind. He said that when his behaviors had no effect on me that he saw that he could stay in his own misery and decline, or he needed to do something about it. In his words he said he heard me saying, "It's my way or the highway". I never told him that and I was not going to leave but, in his mind, he had two choses, which he explained, either to be in misery or make changes so he could relate to me. It is good to have a satisfying relationship now, although I found it does not influence my level of happiness and joy. An awakened life is self-sustaining and filled with riches from within. You supply your own light and love, and another is frosting on the cake, as we say in the USA.

With an awakened perspective, you can return love for non-love, as well. The negative behavior simply does not register in your reality. This is one of the greatest contributions you can give to another.

Please do not misinterpret what I am saying. If you are in an abusive relationship, please seek safety and professional counseling. Respect is an integral part of relating. Some relationships are not meant to continue.

How does my awakening experience play into how I relate to others now? I will give you a step-by-step breakdown, as I've lost my ability to analyze with acquiring my operating state of flow.

    I will relate what I learned in that other dimensional experience. I am not a body; I am an energy pattern in a sea of energy that is power and love. There are dimensions beyond this Earth life. The love I felt was profound and went straight to my core. I found I am valued and cared for, far beyond my wildest imagination.

    I don't feel that I am my body. I relate from a firm center and that firm center is open and engaged. It is much easier than having a self-image to have to support at every turn. Yet it has its own challenges, like being open to the unknown daily. I relate to each person moment to moment and listen to what they have to say, caring for them and saying a thing or two. My family is near and dear to my heart, and I spend a good amount of time relating to them and investing in their lives with caring. I iron out conflicts with love, sensitivity, and honesty, on my part. I allow the other person to have their own opinions and beliefs plus come from how conscious they view things. I meet a stranger or two and invite them to coffee, on occasion. The big difference now is that my heart is very open and that is where I relate from.

    Love is the ultimate gift. I rips everything wide open, from hearts, to personally evolving, to relationships, to compassion for self and another, to exploding beauty, to the juice that makes the world rich. It brings us to our knees before the altar of our true nature.

DISCOVERING YOUR TRUE NATURE

Our true nature is not definable. We would like to understand it with our finite mind but cannot because it is infinite and all potential. When we are in our true nature then we are in a higher realm, once we strip away the untruths that we have bought in to, that always cause conflict in our lives. This is stripped of identity, of a puffed-up sort. In my true nature, I experience myself as a powerful unseen consciousness with my uniqueness retained, i.e., talents to enjoy and share.

The current operating model in the World is the use of body, emotions, and intellect. However, there are realms that are more refined and rewarding. Our true nature is full of love, vibrancy, clear seeing and actions that flow from being a part of the higher realm. Then body, emotions and intellect are tools of my true nature, to be used in relating and doing in my Earthly life. This higher realm is not separate from but a part of Earthly life. An example of that would be how the two-dimensional world is part of the three-dimensional world.

I would like to share an experience I had of my true nature. In 2012, at the age of 64, I was unexpectedly given an awakening experience. The same one that many ascetics and holy persons have, I read about many such after my experience. Specifically, Adyashanti in his book 'The End of Your World' describes his. The properties and qualities that I experienced were shocking, in a good way. All the space was filled with love and power, and it went straight through me. I was a conscious entity without bodily sensations, although I was still in the body. I felt the most real and authentic me that I ever have ever felt, it spoke to my core. A voice spoke to me and said that 'I have been with you through everything that you have gone through', with the utmost love and caring feelings that went with it. I was consumed with wonder and joy. This all communicated to my very core/essence.

Before this experience, I had no idea of this realm, the properties thereof or where I fit in to it. I know this is a radical example of finding things out that you never imagined about your true nature. On a spiritual path, snippets of this are given along the way. These are unexpected and wondrous. They speak to a deep place within you, thus motivating you to uncover more and more of your true nature. As you do proceed, there are many things to say goodbye to and many surprises that will take getting used too. Be patient with yourself and know although sometimes you feel like you are on another planet that it is a part of a vaster realm that you have just not experienced until now. It takes some getting used to, because it directly flies in the face of body, emotions and intellect and the emphasis on that that you have been conditioned too. As you dissolve more and more illusions/delusions you will find that you no longer have a use for them. Then little by little you will be introduced to more refined interactions and experiences.

I remember, after a heart opening transitional period, I went shopping at Walmart. I decided to practice seeing others from the deep heart level that I had just uncovered within myself. As I walked around, I look into each person's essence, far different than their physical appearance, and it enthralled me. I quit shopping and just walked around in awe and with each person it started consuming me with joy, more and more. This happened to such an extent, that I started to go into my awakening experience again. This was another deep exposure to the realm of my true nature.

Over the years I have unloaded so many false beliefs, some painfully I might add, that have bit by bit uncovered my true nature. I have found that it is loving, vibrant, clear seeing, creative and silently powerful. I do not feel a part of Earthly commonly held beliefs. My seeing is far different, I focus on what is in front of me but with clear vision, i.e. like seeing the essence of others and appreciating it to the point of joy or when someone is unloving to be able to see it is an out of place behavior, it does not register within my system. Yes, I feel the pull of old behaviors in myself, but I recognize them, and I can see them for what they are as well. Living in your true nature is living a high-quality life beyond the norms of what is currently known.

There are higher realms to our life here on Earth. They cannot be defined because they operate by properties that we currently do not have language for. However, we can live in these higher realms plus use our Earthly gifts of body, emotions, and intellect as an adjunct to our true nature. It is certainly not common. The payoff is found in each individual being their true nature and the more rewarding and refined life this affords. It is felt each minute, as you live it. Then it naturally radiates out to others and all aspects of this Earth life.

SPIRIT PULLS YOU ASIDE TO REVEAL DIAMONDS

At times we are individually thrust into alone time. Each one of us will have times when the external circumstances catch us so far off guard that we are reduced to just living and nothing else makes sense. We cannot even relate to anything external. We might not know how we can go on. This takes us to a new level of self that we might not have known was this deep. True it is wanting but remains carved out.

These inward times are rich with the potential to learn something that has been tripping us up and we didn't know it. The deep dive into self is taken, in the first place, because somewhere in our belief system our wires were crossed, when the beliefs were developed. I will give a simple example of this in my life, growing up I saw relationships in movies where the ideal of everyone getting along happened. When I first fell in love and married, I thought this was the way it would be. It soon became apparent that this was far from the truth. My therapist diagnosed me as 'reaction adjustment to adult life'. In other words, I was not prepared for adult life. When we form beliefs, if they are not on solid ground, then they are cross wired, and we will get shocked at some point. We all get our wires crossed with false beliefs, as we grow up and then proceed into adulthood.

In hopes of illuminating the subject, I will relate a difficult event that happened to me recently. A family member was hospitalized, a serious chronic condition. I went into stress, and it drove me to that alone place inside myself. Where there are no answers. I kept up my morning spiritual/personal growth studies. Not wanting to be under stress, knowing that my mind was just racing in circles, and I was out of sync with myself, I was reminded of my most essential precious nature, my center. It was calling to me and I went there. I returned to my true nature, from the stress and aloneness. I was then able to be that essential self, separate from the outside stress of the situation. My wires had been crossed in letting external events and players pull me out of my true nature. Upon rectifying that, by returning to my true nature, I found I could empathize and contribute much more effectively, in my loved one's situation.

This poem came out of that:

PROCEED

My heart
Sees
Beyond
What
My eyes
Can

Extending
Out
In all directions

Touching
Fathomless
Outreaching

Purity
Tender
Nectar
Resides
At center
Within

Ability
To
Remain

Relish
The center
That is.
Felt

Extends
In all
Directions
Delightfully

Patience
Clarity
Love
With anything
Encountered

Noticeable
Contact
When meeting with
Limited insight

Yet it still
Encompasses
Runs through
With delight
An ordinary encounter

Unseen
Lights
Flash
Illuminate

Resting
Modulating
Back and forth
Quietly

Satisfied
Replenished

Able to proceed

    It took the stress of the difficult situation to put me in an alone time that was fraught with anxiety. Then I remembered my true nature, which I have been educated on most intensely in the last 11 years. There have been a couple poignant encounters, in my spiritual journey, that have touched the sweet alive core that I am that have shown to me my essential self. They spoke to the deepest me. I went to that sweet pure place inside of me.

I wrote the above poem upon my return, from stress/aloneness to true nature. I do not live the intensity of this poem in my daily life but a calmer more 'put one foot in front of the other' version. I still exude from my center and receive in my heart, just quietly.

Perspective, to know the truth more and more with greater and greater insight. There is dismantling false concepts, through your chosen method or the method that finds you. Then being given clear vision to see what is real. By and by it becomes more apparent until you are unable to deny it and desire to live it more and more. You see it as true, although it seems quite unbelievable to your logical mind. You are a slice of something you know not but you do know that it is real and glorious.

TO BE HELD IN THE BOSOM OF ETERNITY

TO BE HELD IN THE BOSOM OF ETERNITY AND SEE WITH CLEAR VISION

That would be wonderful if we could do that and live with others that were of like orientation.

Starting with me. Being held in the bosom of eternity, pure love, and seeing clearly, self-awareness that radiates out, came in fits and starts, over about 11 years. I had not crossed the line of continuously living it in my everyday life. Which I continuously longed to do and was on a steep spiritual/personal growth learning curve. Although you cannot order these things, I felt I was opening more and more areas within myself.

Then I came to a point in my life where I felt I could live my true nature, love and self-awareness, in my daily life. By feeling capable and ready, it is always followed by me experiencing what is standing in my way of doing whatever the task is at hand, my inner fears. Please bear with me in relating a dream I had that illustrates my inner fears in putting these newfound capabilities in to practice. Don't expect it to make sense, none of our fears do, because they are based on our survival instinct and not what is present.

I was at a gorgeous holiday location with friends and relatives. We went on a scenic tour. The vistas were stunning and truly consumed me. Overtaken with joy and the nonstop splendor, I was lost in a state of bliss and peace for hours on end. Dusk was approaching, I needed to switch to another bus to go back to my lodging. Watching that bus leave in another direction, I ran after it, my belongings barely escaped being swept away as I ran. I took the wrong route on foot and missed my ride back. I had to return to my present tour vehicle. I was with relatives that disapproved of me anyway and I would now be humiliated, because of my childish lack of focus which resulted in missing my return bus. In a panic, I imagined being stranded on the large boulders at the seafront with the cold waves crashing upon them throughout the night.

In my morning studies the following day, I saw that I was at a demarcation point of insanity! (a little humor there). Rather, a demarcation point of living my true nature, with joy and wonder in my daily life. Knowing, come what may, I would be risking life & limb and humiliation, my fears. I knew once implemented; I was not coming back. I entertainingly thought, if I did take this leap and I was caught in the same dream then I could write a note to myself to catch the last bus out, probably not.

With my fears addressed, I implemented my capabilities to live in self-awareness, being held in the bosom of eternity and seeing clearly. I did catch when, along the way, my fears started to arise within me, and I saw they were not real and proceeded on in my newfound freedom, to my ongoing delight.

I wrote this poem:

AWARENESS

Love spoke
To the deepest deep
I knew
We were the same

Beauty
Stalked me
I
Melted

Power persisted
Ever revealing
Its' truth
Particularly to me

All leaving
A trace
Of my presence
In awareness

    Your true nature is self-aware and living in the bosom of eternity and has clear vision. It is being you and at the same time fully immersed in the energies of the universe. Naturally in wonder, being love itself and at the same time being a part of the far scope of the universe.

HEART POWER

It is only by being in our hearts that we have power. Don't ask me how or why. I did not make up the rules or, more to the point, what my true nature is composed of.

How did I find this out? Not by any conventional means, I assure you. It started with my awakening experience and then was reinforced by afterwork until I gradually came to believe and accept it through application in my life. Like, it really worked and was proven true in my mind and heart.

My introduction to the depth and magnitude of my heart was shown to me in my awakening experience. I wrote a poem about it, and I think it will illustrate my mind set, the depth of the experience and how it affected me.

TOGETHER

I walk
In a
Forest green
Deep

No light
Deep brush surrounding
Occasional eyes
Peering

Eking out
An existence

A bird
Alights
On my shoulder
An unspoken treasure

Then suddenly
I am present
No body feeling
Like all I am is
Myself
More aware
Than aware

Yet every inch
Is permeated
With love
And immense
Presence

I ask
Why I was
Given this

Spoken without words,
"I have been
With you
Every moment"

My heart
Swelled
Then Flooded,
To the
Absolute depth
Of my being

My heart
And the breadth
Of the message
Laced together

    The next significant heart opening came in the form of a course that I took that exposed a deep wound that I had. Through that work I was able to reconcile it to see the truth of where I misinterpreted the event, and subsequently carried that programming on into my life for the next 50 years, to one degree or another. I applied this awareness to my life and was able to eventually overcome the maladjusted behaviors, for example, attention getting. Through this heart opening I could now experience more of the richness in human relationships, often without saying a word.

    How did I come to embrace and live the truth of pure heart and presence. It was a contemplative process and application of possible truths, to see if they resonated with me and worked in everyday life. For example, how can heart be so powerful when it is a place of vulnerability? I tried it out. I shut up and sank into my heart and related from there in different circumstances. It worked! I felt empowered and empowered others with my attitude. This is my contemplative/application process that I use.

Further affirmation came in knowing that this heart connection was me, inextricably a part of all life, as it flows through me, and I delight in it. For example, when I witness suffering and pain, I am able to hold others in my heart and serve with emotional and physical boundaries. This heart awareness/power is who I am, it is my bedrock. I am home inside of me, even in difficult circumstances.

On my part, it has been an exposure, contemplating, healing, and application process, with a heck of a lot of support from others and spirit. Letting go of what I thought I was and incorporating what I find is true in me. I have taken you on my trajectory and I fully support and encourage you in yours. No walk is the same. I know you will find much truth along the way and live more and more in your heart awareness which is where your power is and connection to the universe, your true nature.

THERE IS NO DEATH, ONLY NEW BEGINNINGS

This past week, I had an unfortunate thing occur to me. My husband passed on. It has been a long time coming but the absence of someone you love is not something you can prepare for.

I have been very fortunate, the level of support and outpouring of love that has been shown to me was needed and soothingly received by myself. I have not suffered.

My alone moments are quiet and peaceful. I know I am starting a new phase of my life, that I am slipping in to. I have not welcomed it yet but am on this ride with an open heart and willing spirit.

At this point, my mind cannot think or analyze due to present circumstances, grieving for the loss of my best friend. I have chosen to share a poem that I wrote during my spiritual studies this week.

RESIDE

Every waft of breeze a
Caresses
The treetops
Sending them
Into ripples
Patterns

Administering
Ramparts of delight
Scattered
Yet forming

Against a clouded
Brilliant panorama
Enough in its
Own right

I can only perceive
One at a time

And then
On to the next

Ever forming
A whole
Where I reside

    There is no suffering in your true nature. I am thankful to be able to partake of that. Thank you for your kind wishes for me. I am overwhelmingly grateful. I celebrate life and love and you are a part of that.

PURE PRESENCE

Living in the now is a much sought after state. The magic is found in taking this from an intellectual concept to a living breathing presence of yourself, no overlays, opinions, analysis, or heavy emotions. Being present in a pure form and being so integrally apart of existence that you realize you are the same as. Like this vibrating alive transparent screen that is so embedded in the now, that there is no difference in perception between outer and inner. Yet you as an entity are alive and accounted for with all senses and feelings online. You are an alive breathing, perceiving presence with no overlays. You are out of the 'normal' negative imposing earthy experience, although you can still perceive its presence. You are primarily a receiving entity and able to act when necessary. Peace and joy pervade in this state, although many other emotions pass through.

You might be thinking, I'm in the now and yet I am not able to feel this peace and joy you speak of. What am I missing, you ask. My response is, a lot. Specifically, the components that make up your true nature. Somewhere along the way, you discarded a component or two that is essential for experiencing your true nature. You have overcompensated or undercompensated from a perceived lack within you. You were threatened and went into fight or flight mode, unconsciously out of defense, in order to seek the love and safety that you deserved. You gave up all or parts of your true nature. Which you really didn't give up, more like you buried them beneath all that overlay of efforting or non efforting. There are many different systems and disciplines that explain this basic conflict that we fall in to and also how to resolve it. I encourage you to find the one that best resonates with you.

Through decades of removing these overlays I concluded, through irrefutable evidence, that this was indeed where I resided. This took years and years of seeing through multiple layers and applying my insights. This did give a clear path for me to resolve in my journey to my true nature. I had glimpses of my true nature along the way from deep inward turnings or spiritual experiences that I was granted, as well.

Knowing something intellectually and living it are two completely different things. Through gradually seeing my true nature and finding safety in that I did take the final plunge, stepping into my true nature and living from there every day. This took a conscious effort and a consenting on my part. You must see the truth and agree to be it. I've heard it called 'the dark night of the soul'. You and you alone need to make that decision and consent to step into that unknown of a completely new way of being. The same principle applies here as in Yoda's training of Skywalker in The Empire Strikes back. Yoda stated, "You must unlearn what you have learned" & "Do or do not. There is no try." There is no intellectual or emotional overlay, just BE and interact with what is there from that. It takes directly being in this state of immersion, like chlorine in water, to know of the otherness of who you are and being apart of everything. There are no words for it or any shortcuts. When you are submerged in your true nature, you are a different, more refined alive creature, your authentic self. When lived continuously, at first it is as if you are on another planet and must reorient. Like a baby learning to walk. Then when that passes it becomes deep gratitude and joy with who you truly are and the secure vastness that you are a part of.

If this seems like an arduous journey, it is. However, it is one ripe with great vistas that you could never imagine. Those are the gold nuggets on the way to the gold mine. The life of a seeker is difficult but far more satisfying than not being proactive. Resting in your true nature and being authentic in that rarefied atmosphere is the reward. Side note:

It is not by definition exclusive of Earth life but rather inclusive of Earth life and ever serving the greater good.

SO MUCH MORE

I am here
Clear, Transparent
Yet accounted for

I feel
Touched
Pulled
Grounded

I know
I am
Taken
Care of

Receiving
From source
That is
Apart of me

Spreading
Unseen pearls
Touching
Hearts

Witnessing beauty
At every turn
Resonating as unity

My true nature
That encompasses
So much more

By Audrey Weigel

LIVING IN FLOW

One is invited to be so clear within that you are the same as pure existence. Ramana Maharshi said – It is more accurate to say that you and the void are the same. This is a state of purity, absolute clarity within, with nothing going on but presence of self. I could equate it to being in what used to be referred to as 'the zone', in sports. The qualities are like everything slows down and your perceptions are heightened and open. The process of disassembling concepts serves the end of unveiling the clear self. You remain but are just here with no agenda. One characteristic of it is the 'peace that passeth all understanding' that Christian scriptures speak of.

Heart is also required. Have you ever witnessed an awakened being that did not have joy within themselves and a deep love of others. It is part and parcel to being awakened and living it. Someplace along the way, their hearts were quickened to be aware of their preciousness. This can be attained by healing our wounds, especially our core wounds. After uncovering so much, you, the treasure, shine through. This pulsating alive center, yourself, was always there and needed uncovering. This gives the juice to being awake, brings everything to the forefront and it is viewed as sacred.

Seeing that we are not alone and accepting this is what allows the flow to breathe in and out through you. No one arrives at awakening solely through their own devices. It comes through the guidance of spirit and earthly beings. You could also call the systems of discipline part of this because they are administered by others that know more than we do at that point. So, to continually trust and accept these guides and higher order companionship is required. To the point that you give yourself over to their love and wisdom. To allow this is necessary. One could even take signs, inspiration, and learnings as their spirit guides, if it flows in and out freely.

There are innumerable ways to get in touch with these innate capacities. Each one is right for those individuals' learning propensities. There are logical left brain, intuitive right brain, and contemplative disciplined systems. No need to stay with one system either, I move around according to what I need at that time. For example, when I was younger, I started out with religion. Then to psychotherapy. Then to deep psychological healing groups. Then to my awakening experience, given through no effort of my own. Then more self-directed healing and eastern religions. I have never meditated or done yoga, although I do recommend that it is a way that resonates with you.

With these components in place, presence, heart and allowing flow in and through, you have a good base within yourself for awakening.

Then there is the final plunge, which no one comes back from. It is a decision because you intuitively know what is required and what lies ahead. You know you must let all reasoning, identity, history, the sum of what you thought you were go. This is what is needed to live in an awakened state permanently, not just to visit snippets of it. Then you will find yourself just present and what comes comes and what goes goes. The moment you are experiencing is ordinary and full.

Your senses are heightened. Your heart is open to the subtlest nuances. Mostly it's quiet and you are just bright and present. Interacting with whatever comes along. Using your time for your leanings or serving. Open and thankful to listen to spirit guides, no matter what form they take. Able to recognize negativity as sacred, albeit a coarser form. Absolute trust. Honoring your internal rhythms. Ever so grateful.

GROUNDED
It flows through
Like air on a glass sea
Wild, fresh, grounded
It and I are the same

PLACE
Life is passion
Like the ringing of a bell
It flows through
Loud and clear

The connecting point
Seated within
Deep, Still

A combination of
Presence and Heart

Actively allowing
Flow to have
Its way

Our rightful place

LOVE WRIT LARGE

Love is unity, no separation. Whether it is with a person, sunset, piece of art or an activity. There is a merging where you lose your idea of yourself and merge as one with the person or what you are involved in. It is that touching point that is so delicious and precious.

Speaking of love, relationship with another can be a many splendored thing or a many splintered thing. Usually, a combination of the two. "Marriage is the highest yoga. The shiva-shakti union on earth is the counterpart of divine union." — Yogi Bhajan (found at www.annapurnaliving.com) The road to this union, that Yogi Bhajan speaks of, is fraught with compassion and self-discovery. It is intense because it is up close and personal. Judgements of self and other are exposed, as with self-limiting beliefs. It is all grist for the mill of resolving hidden agendas and self-limitations. Love writ large does not need anything for itself. That's how you can recognize a limiting belief, it is crying out me-me-me. Yes, we do have needs but not to eclipse another's truth or path. The self in union with the universe is self-sustaining. One can maintain equilibrium and grounding with sustenance and communion with guides and the universe. Usually this equilibrium and grounding is hard won through our listening to spirit and being willing to let go of the old self and seeing how we are limiting ourselves. I have found that the stronger the bond between myself and spirit/universe then the more I can love and sustain myself in difficult relationship aspects. Of course in most cases, earthly support is needed if the circumstances are trying. That being said, there is also a natural timing to the beginning and ending of relationships. There is a process of letting go, discarding, and opening our eyes to new possibilities.

Your true nature knows no judgements or limiting beliefs. It is of an entirely different sort than what we know of in everyday accepted living. Eckart Tolle calls it the 'vertical dimension'. I like that because it has a practical flavor to it, functional. It implies a setting apart from the everyday accepted mode, being the horizontal dimension. By gradually seeing the falseness of judgements and beliefs and applying these insights into our lives we come to live this vertical dimension. We have released the hold that the horizontal dimension has on us. We see with new eyes. This new dimension is full of heart and truths that you live because you are that. You walk around being these things, love, fascination, grounded involvement, compassion, just because that is what you innately are. You see and feel that you are one with the universe and everything in it, at that point.

PRESENT

I surrender
To the light
That I am

Being conscious
Of
Being conscious

Be
Am
Open

Outside
Inside
Through

Stable
Moving

Receiving
Present

**RESPLENDENT
ACRYLIC PAINTING**

INTEGRATED PEACE

There are interests and areas of life that bring positive experiences. Let's take sailing, to master the craft of sailing and ride the wind with no resistance brings a feeling of unity and peace. It's as if you melt into the moment and ride it endlessly. Or scaling a rock front, all sense of time is lost, and your senses are on high alert, you become one with the moment. Or painting where you step back and plan and then go into the painting process where you lose your sense of separateness and meld into the painting application. When participating in an experience where you are fully engaged, it's as if you disappear and yet are more fully present.

We as humans long for these moments. Whole industries are built up around this longing, for example recreation, hobbies, traveling. You could include work that you love in this. This is our true nature peeking through. You could call these non-experiences, due to disappearing or melting into them because it is as if you are so much a part of it that you disappear.

In spirituality, it is the goal to be in union with the whole, all of creation and potential. All healing schools are designed to resolve inner and outer conflicts and arrive at union. Yoga is the path of the right brain that takes one incrementally to this goal, yang approach. Tantra is the path of the left brain of surrender, yin approach. Then there are western approaches, for example, gestalt is an internal resolution of opposites, inner child hypnotherapy which seeks to resolve conflicts that originated in childhood. They are interested in individual conflict resolution to integration.

Our true nature is integrated with all life and all potential. There is no sense of self but being conscious. You can get a sense of it by being aware of being aware, that stillness. Then multiple that to being present like this throughout your day. This is most often done by using whatever method of discipline or healing that fits your individual makeup and coming in to a more and more integrated state. For myself, I have used many different healing modalities and disciplines. I used the left-brain approach of inquiry and deep subconscious healing, which led me to the right brain approach, surrender. Now it is being smack dab in the middle of everything and appreciating and receiving. I respond or don't respond according to the circumstances and what I feel moved to do.

After all the work of clearing outdated beliefs, we have our free will to decide if we want to fully submit to the position of being so much a part of the whole that we disappear, fully awake, like a piece of melted chocolate being put into a vat of melted chocolate. This greater arena is all of creation and all potential. This is what you are in your true nature. It is felt at the levels of mind, heart, and body. You are still present, more than ever before. The tables are turned from action to receiving and then seeing if you are motivated to act. You see everybody and everything as sacred and doing their thing just fine without you. Bad or evil is seen as distorted thinking, conflict to be worked out, although it does evoke sadness and heartache to watch.

The downside of describing this is head tripping it and trying to replicate this in your mind and step into the role. It cannot be replicated. That is why sages point to it and do not describe it. You can only get there by taking the journey of self-discovery and then making the final decision to melt into the whole.

Arduous? Yes. That's why they say it takes lifetimes. I believe that you can do it in one lifetime. The support is all around, magazines, groups, even on YouTube now. You can be an everyday person and achieve it through intention, reflection, hard work, and discipline. Are you fed up with the ups and downs of this life and the false promises that it held out to you? Then you are ready to embark on this path to absolute fulfillment and integrated peace. I lend a big hand and hug of support to you.

SERENDIPITOUS SURRENDER

We have been inculcated to revere the proactive approach, the opposite of surrender. Not that that is incorrect, but I see great value in the submissive, accepting approach as well. Yes, I did discover this accidentally. Through a misguided childhood experience, I came to revere and employ the proactive 'go getter' approach throughout my life. It is only serendipitously that I came to appreciate and employ the submissive, accepting approach as well. This was brought to me from the many healings and learnings that I have went through and then employed those openings and insights in my life.

Going back in history, an ancient Chinese philosophy, found in the Oxford dictionary: Yang being the active male principle of the universe, characterized as male and creative and associated with heaven, heat, and light. Yin being the passive female principle of the universe, characterized as female and sustaining and associated with earth, dark, and cold. Chinese philosophy gives equal due to both yang and yin.

One of the hallmarks of a person living in their true nature is an absolute commitment to truth, above their own personal feelings and ideas. This is a yin principle because it is primarily being humble and accepting of the truth. Often this is disorienting and confusing because it flies in the face of what you have known. Still truth is truth and must be accepted and lived, submission to truth. When I embarked on this journey, it was for healing and then it became for Christ consciousness, a positive orientation in life, and now it is living my true nature. Each one of those steps had purpose and took recognition of a truth greater than I was living at that moment. I had to surrender to the new truth that I saw and apply it in my life, no matter what my perceived objections were. Though it was frightening at times, diving in to the unknown, I knew that that was the only way forward to new and fresh territory in my life, so I submitted to it. It usually took me awhile to let it all sink in and then awhile to implement the new truth. As time went on, it became more familiar and doable. Then applying it in my life and working out the kinks in the application.

The further and further I proceeded then the further and further my ideas and feelings about myself and all around me dissolved. Because those ideas and feelings about myself were acquired, not who I am. When I came down to my basic being, there was no description and merely presence, then a big question popped up. Now who am I and where do I go from here? Fortunately, there was a sense of far beyond and a door there. That door went to the embrace of my being in the flow and companionship of the universe. Again, this is a yin skill to know the truth and submit to it, surrender. This was difficult because I had to agree to give up control and be a part of something greater and unknown. I stepped through that doorway, and I reap rewards through true companionship and continual learning now.

We might think this happens in some far-off place, but it is all right here and now. A Buddhist Monk once thumped his walking stick on the ground and told his students that it is all happening right here and now. They were bewildered. I experienced this, the more my feelings and ideas of myself dissolved then the more present in my true nature and connected to the myriad positive aspects of life I became. Living an authentic life automatically has eyes, deep connectivity to all about. We are enamored with life and love because that is the substance of our true nature and presence. Make no mistake, besides knowing you belong to the heart of everything, you do retain those leanings of your being, for example, your flavor of serving others.

Surrendering is necessary to learning, moving more and more towards your true nature and living your true nature. Learning never stops. Bowing to a new truth, bowing to a new lifestyle, bowing to a new healing method, bowing to love, bowing to responsibility, bowing to fun, bowing to a relationship, etc., all necessary. Bowing to a universe that knows more.

VICTIMHOOD VS FREEDOM

Not much hope going around these days. Most folks are caught up in the doom and gloom of this sphere. There seems to be a lot of it. It is easy to get entangled in this pervasive thinking. It is the topic of everyday conversation, that is not even considering our routine way of thinking and feeling. The mindset is that the odds are stacked against us. This leads to feeling weighted down, trudging along or fighting one unending battle after another. It is dampening to our attitude towards love and life. Indeed, it is like throwing a wet blanket on our hopes and dreams. It appears to control different aspects of our lives.

My beloved late husband said, if he had a problem then all he had to do was go look in the mirror. This is not just a pep talk on his part but an orientation that proves out in practice. How many times have you had an insurmountable problem that burdened you for long periods and then to work it out and to become better for it. That's speaking from an individual point of view and not the general environment. But that is all we have jurisdiction over, our own outlook.

Sometimes it is helpful to take a subject to the extreme to sort out the components. An extreme case can be found in Victor Frankl's book, Man's Search for Meaning. He was a WW2 POW; his life was under the control of his captors. Yet, he found that he could control one thing, his personal beliefs, and this made all the difference. He was able to retain his sense of self and what life meant to him in these dire circumstances. This is told in the Bible story of Joseph being a prisoner of the king in Egypt, as well. He retained his faith and beliefs. In both these cases, the prisoners were not victims but retained their freedom, the freedom within.

The freedom they had came from a deep belief in themselves and the truths that they believed in, regardless of their circumstances. These truths they had, that they stood on, did not come by happenstance but by deep inner reflection and/or knowledge of truth when it appeared. They were not victims but found deeper truths that they owned.

I have found that the views circulating around are limited and that there are far greater pastures. Ignorance, a lack of knowledge, pervades. As I grew up, I bought in to the common view and then had to reassess and implement a wider perspective that was more congruous with my true nature. There are many different healing systems, both Eastern and Western. The different healing systems are more compatible with some individuals than others. I suggest trying out the different methodologies and seeing which speaks to you. But to be sure, a deconstruction of previous limited beliefs is needed.

With this reintroduction to other parts of my true nature, I found more authenticity and freedom. These are hallmarks of coming closer to living the full-blown model of your true self. Then it shook down to applying that new knowledge in my life, being open to other ways as they present themselves, for example, choosing new friends, changing jobs, new interests, a different attitude born from processing. Implementing these new ways was a learning in itself, it brought up the blocks that had been there all along that had prevented me from engaging in these healthier alternatives. By working through the implementation, it anchored in the new learning.

As time goes on, processing or discovering what is true for you, will take a positive toll. It will be felt on three different levels, your mind, heart, and body. In my case, it worked on different aspects at different times. Then eventually, it all came together, as a fully functioning instrument. My mind was clear, my heart actively feeling, and my body open to universal flow. All in all you will feel deeply loved and connected to all of life, minus ignorance. These will be your instruments inside of you that will be utilized by the flow of your being, true nature. These honed skills just naturally develop as you take responsibility for your victimhood and move more and more towards your true nature, your freedom.

Through decades of processing and being given continual support, from mentors and spirit, I have worked through many obstacles to arrive at peace and joy. Side note: some people can just see truth and follow it but that was not the case for me.

There are two things I am most thankful for, the love I have received/the love I have given and, as the Buddhist saying goes 'you never crossed the same river twice', learning and experiencing whole new areas of my life. Now with me, it is all a wide free open plane and I am so much at peace that I hardly know what to do with myself.

I send you all the love I can muster and wish for you freedom and enjoyment. Your true nature is not in some far-off place but right here, fully engaged in life.

Remember:

You are braver than you believe,
stronger than you seem,
smarter than you think and twice
as beautiful as you'd ever imagined.
Rumi

EXUDING PRESENCE

Being present is a sought-after art.

So many distractions, that take us away from the present moment. Often the present moment seems boring, without distractions of some sort, as well. In contrast, childhood engagement was creative and fascinating. For example, making forts with passageways out of large cardboard boxes. Why the disparity between childhood and adulthood? What was lost or found in the interim? I see that we lost our innocent engagement with the present and acquired a new set of interests that took us away from the present moment. Yes, we need to engage in an adult world but why do we have to lose engagement with the wonders of the present? For example, how our loved one's voice lilts or the smell of moisture in the air in the forest.

At what frequency do we start to hear, see, and feel the present moment? The frequency of the Earth, what pulsates and is emitted by the Earth, is 7.83 hertz. That is 7.8 3 cycles per second. This was discovered by Otto Schumann in the 20th century and is called Schumann's resonance. It is a very low electromagnetic frequency that runs through and protects the living things on this planet. The Earth, through our experiences with nature, sooth, comfort and give an excellent atmosphere to ponder or meditate. When we come into or engineer these lower frequencies in our body we naturally come into synchronicity with what is, the present moment.

When we are children we acquire wounding from various sources, through no fault of our own. My psychotherapist said that everyone has some kind of wound, he gave the example of being weaned. These wounds put our focus more outward and cause internal conflicts that we carry through subsequent childhood and adulthood like the need to please others. Mine was a case of not trusting my own judgement and overachieving. There is a whole list of ways a child can be wounded. Basically, when they do not feel safe, secure and loved, then they feel they have to seek that out in different ways, according to their own unique wounding and reaction. This produces tension and takes one out of a calmer frequency, therefore we see much anxiety in individuals and society as a whole.

In many disciplines these woundings are thought of in different ways and their method of readdressing it varies. The individual temperament and what suits it best, has to be considered as well. It has to do with raising one's frequency from lower to higher, as in the chakra system. Christian religion would take the approach of overcoming sins or transgressions. Basically, in order to be free enough to live in the present moment you need to be clear your availability to enjoy the moment. This entails not being consumed with the lower frequency activities, for example addictions, holding grudges, having excessive appetites for anything. Woundings put our focus outwards and our inner life is overlooked. Side note: what is referred to as a higher frequency in spiritual circles is actually a lower frequency electromagnetic hertz vibration. One is calmer and more in touch with their surroundings and all of life.

As we recognize our reactions and activities that supersede our inner life then we can use the healing systems to gradually eliminate them. Of course, they always have a voice, but it is recognized as an old false recording and put it in the background, mindfulness. As our path unfolds, specifically addressing what we came here to learn, we become freer and feel lighter. We are raising our frequency and more light comes into our being, unlocking pent up invigorating energy that we had long ago locked away. Side note: Look at the major events in your life and what you learned from them, and you can figure out what you came to learn.

At a high frequency, when we have stepped into our true nature, we exude light from the universe, through our true nature and out into the world. This light is drawn into our being because our frequency has shed so much and can now reside in its true nature where universal light flows through. This is usually a long gradual process marked with insights and glimpses of what your true nature feels like. Then one day we make a choice to fully step into the light and give up all that we have learned- to stand naked, with no ego, and be a part of the entire wonderful vastness of love and power.

We are all light beings that reside at high frequencies and universal energy flows through us. At this point, others can easily recognize what you exude. What you are and exude is different from the bogged down energy that is the norm in society and others really want to be happy and free themselves. Yes, it markedly stands out and it is not necessary to express it in words. Of course, it will depend on another's receptivity to those frequencies that you now emit. Many will be so closed off that they do not even recognize these frequencies, but they will in their hearts.

The dictionary talks about 'being' in terms of 'alive and real'. When you shed all but the ground floor of who you are then you have returned to what is alive and real. It is possible in this life, but it takes dedication and courage. A practice or discipline to assist you, is needed as well. For instance, morning spiritual study and meditation and attending workshops. Or ongoing attendance with a healing practitioner or group. Or regular attendance at religious meetings with side studies.

We have come to a place in society today where spiritual practice is accepted and widespread. This was not the case 50 years ago when the Maharishi introduced meditation in the USA. There is now a plethora a disciplines to choose from. Some of these are mainstream religion, healing practices, psychotherapy, Hinduism, Buddhism, astrology, tarot, yoga, to name a few.

Living in the moment is a current topic of conversation and is a quality of anyone living in their true nature and not distracted by misguided interests. Loving the whole of it, crying at the definite sad parts and reveling in the joyful. Being in your true nature, presence, is where you know that the concerns of this life are not real. You know that love and love of life are where the juice of life is and you live in it. Those are the only true and permanent parts and there you remain. You actually have no choice but to remain there because that is all your true nature is made of.

Serving the whole by being in your true nature, thereby exuding your presence, is the greatest gift you can give yourself and the world. From there on, if you feel moved to contribute more then please do so. I am doing this with my writing and my family life, presently. Then there is the bursting forth in life that I am currently experiencing. Last week I took a class on an opera soon to be performed in my city. Each day is an adventure. Seems there isn't any night or day but an endless string of interesting activities with a good amount of spiritual study time. I encourage you to follow unwinding your conundrums and living your happiness to the thorough satisfaction of living in your unique true nature.

LIVING LOVE

The title is 'living love'. This is a verb and not a noun. I live love as part of my being that is operative, in my programming and function. I think this must seem antithetical to this modern world of ours, wrought with all manner of disturbing behaviors. Even though it seems paradoxical, it is actually quite natural.

Let's talk about the love part first. How did I come upon this? I will preface this by saying that everyone does it in their own unique way. My story is that I was raised by very moral dedicated parents but in an atmosphere absent of emotion and expressions of love. I knew that I was loved but it was never expressed. Being a sensitive child, I shut down my emotions and went down the path of achievement, hence my driven nature. Through years of healing, I was able to clear my anxieties, overthinking and driven nature. But still my heart was only open when big circumstances came along, not every day. I took a course targeting the opening of the heart and this brought an opening to let love in and it consumed me. It was actually four deep heart opening experiences that finally opened my heart. These experiences went to the core of me, and all left their imprint until I knew my heart was a deep integral part of me.

I now know life from my heart and my solar plexus, that part of your body from below your rib cage to your abdomen including your perineum. Your solar plexus is considered your power center. About the head center, Carl Jung said that your head is only good for balancing your check book, in other words it only has a minimal amount of use in your life. Modern society has gone into overdrive when it comes to the use of the intellect. However, I see your head as part of a receiving and broadcasting station of higher frequency communications, like from and to spirit guides.

Now to come to the living part of 'living love'. You have cleared or are working on clearing the muck away. The muck is that stuff you made up in your head, heart and power center, what you had bought in to in the collective for all those years and practiced it in your life. You have set strong intention to clear all this muck from your life and nothing will stop you. You receive glimpses of the freedom and wonder that you are working towards, seen in small or large ways. You used the practice or practices that best suited your progress. You little by little or all at once saw the truth of your being and put it into practice. You held allegiance to truth above all else.

All along, when I processed and found a new truth about myself about life then I put it into practice in my daily life. This way I worked out the kinks. Like I came up against my fears and saw if it was a go or needed to be refined more. Truth about self and life is in sync with daily life. It makes you freer and happier, in small or big ways. For example, fourteen years ago I was laid off from my job as a nurse for a reason that I did not consider substantial enough. I needed to process my bitter feelings and feel what was the next step. I was surprised to find that my feelings were to retire, I was already breeding german shepherd dogs but it was not enough to sustain me. An online job being a sales agent for my daughters company turned up a few months after that. It took me processing and standing my ground, of retiring, in my daily life for the new level of freedom and happiness to show up. This was a mundane example but can be applied to a more emotionally based realization, as well. Here's a little melodrama for you, the man I fell in love with has an avoidant attachment style. I discovered that I have an anxious attachment style. When he kept going hot and cold per his leanings on committing, I would get anxious. It was the only thing in my life that pulled me out of spirituality, of course, because it was an attachment. He recognizes his buttons and is approaching it. I am able to process mine and am able to love him where he is at. I have gained more freedom and happiness in my own life. It takes not only learning but applying what you learn.

As we dismantle our conditioning, and apply the knowledge we gain in our daily life, then that principle learned can manifest in our daily life. This living love is felt inside us as love of self and happiness of existing. This outpours to others as a joy in living life and compassion for their walk. The trick is that you have to open your heart with your practice and then apply that new vulnerability in your daily life. Otherwise you are just head tripping life and there is no joy in that. I celebrate your walk and especially your personal authenticity and vulnerability to life, where the sweetness is.

NON-ATTACHMENT

I believe that in Western society, the Eastern principle of non-attachment has gotten a bad rap. It is misinterpreted as not caring. When in fact, it is the ultimate in compassion. In truth, standing back in one's essence seeing others and life for what it is gives a clear perspective, a good foundation. In other words, one is not colored by their own views. When we see clearly and observe suffering then we are naturally compassionate and service flows from that.

By definition, one's own essence stands back from the goings on in the world, as it is commonly known. Your essence, and mine, are part of the bedrock of creation and not the accepted drives and concerns that circulate in this present world of ours. We are observers, at our foundation, first and foremost. Take the workings of the Hindu concept of 'sat-chit-ananda.' This is a Hindu concept that represents: I AM – I KNOW I AM – LOVE. The first part is 'sat', I AM. The idea can be taught but must be experienced. It is only in direct experience of the being of ourselves that we know it is ourselves, I AM. Then the second part is 'chit' which is inherent in the I AM, that we experience the I AM and we know it is I. It just comes along with it when we are in our essence, that we feel and know in every part of our being that we are. Then the last part 'ananda', love for everything within and without is a welling up of one's heart with the knowing. I see this as falling in love with the 10,000 things, from the Buddhist tradition. One is so settled into being and the appreciation of the 10,000 things that love naturally flows. To get a clear view, we take our blinders off, find ourselves as I AM, know we are that I AM being, and just love being and everything about us, moment by moment. These qualities are inherent in the experience.

When one can be seated and live from your central place of I AM then one can clearly see others as their I AM and distinguish when they speak of what is not their I AM, thereby seeing with compassion where they strive for happiness, the state of I AM being. This might seem like a narrow perspective, however, it is my belief that true happiness cannot be felt until we uncover our essential nature which is being, the I AM state that unfolds the knowing and love. There are still problems and dilemmas, but we have a clear perspective and do not get caught in them.

The thorn in our sides is the inability to grasp happiness due to the judgments and concepts we are told and buy into. These we have heaped upon ourselves and it nearly sucks the life out of us. As seen by many who just give up in their boxed-in world. No judgment with that, I was caught in these same snares. When these things dissolve, then we can by and by get a clearer view of our being. There are innumerable ways to dissolve this. It is a steep climb up a mountain but can be attained with enough commitment.

I have found that an unexplainable part of being is love. One feels joy at just the fact that I AM, a present stable aware being. Then one naturally falls in love with everything within and without, not needing to possess but accepting everything as it is. Hence, compassion is naturally forthcoming. A paradox, detached in my own essence yet intimately connected through love and compassion.

We are given glimpses of this, which motivates us, "There must be something more than this dreary life that brings never-ending longing and no lasting satisfaction." That is how this life is set up, to have you search within for what is lasting and brings true joy. The deeper we delve, the more in touch with this we come. Non-attachment is the discovery of our simple I AM state that is the bedrock of your existence, no overlays. Compassion just naturally comes forth from this.

It is a journey of self-discovery and giving up control to the evidence of experiencing your being. You start in a narrow circle, and then it becomes ever wider until you know you are, and it encompasses you. I extend my utmost love to you on this path and tell you that it is so worth it.

RESTORED

Why do I need the promise of the passing sun
When each moment stands for itself
One moment appreciated
Can never compare to a piped dream
Acceptance that I am
My knowing that I am
Ignites the fire
Sight restored

ON THE SUBJECT OF ENLIGHTENMENT

EMBODY WHAT YOU LEARN

It's simply not practical and effective to learn something and not embody it. Embodying it means thoroughly incorporating it into your life, to the point of having it resonate throughout your being. The sweetness and rewards of learning are felt in your body.

What is there to learn? If you are not happy and fulfilled down deep inside then you have some things to learn. Happiness is the nature of your true being.

When I was young, I thought adults acted strangely, and I could not make sense of their behavior. I vowed to figure that out. I made learning human nature and existential questions the focus of my life. Now, after many years, I know why adults act like they do, and I still think they behave strangely. I have largely figured out the answers to my existential questions, although it has led to many more questions.

I propose that as you learn through the problems you encounter in life you can approach your true nature and then embrace it. Problems come in all forms, such as employment, relationships, illness, etc. I will give a method to solve problems that I have used my whole life and it has served me well.

STEPS IN INTERNAL OR EXTERNAL CONFLICT RESOLUTION:

RECOGNIZE that I have a problem. I need to be compassionate to myself, and I need to sort through my feelings. It doesn't matter if no one else can understand my feelings and desires; these are mine to feel and be compassionate to myself about.

STUDY out a solution. In some cases, it would take a period of study and using resources.

PICK THE BEST SOLUTION. It might be one of many that you have looked into. It needs to be something you are motivated by and invested in. Sometimes, it is the best of two unwelcome solutions.

IMPLEMENTATION. Incorporate it into your life, all at once or incrementally. This can be anxiety-producing, to say the least. It is a problem you have, and you are trying a new approach.

GET SUPPORT. For example, from friends or educational materials that you trust. A wise person knows that it is shorter route to get support than not.

RESULTS. See how the implementation worked out, including the pros and cons. Be compassionate with yourself here. This is an experiment in solving your problem. The results are usually unexpected. You might be pleased with the results or need to start again at the first step of RECOGNIZING and go through the process again.

Having the solution resonate in your being is done incrementally and exponentially. At first, you might not even recognize why you are unhappy. And then when you work through the steps, it might take 6 months. Then the result resonates with you, but to a small degree since you still have a long way to go to clear enough space within to let the light shine unimpaired. But you are thankful for the relief and the greater degree of happiness. Then, by and by (this took me decades), as you keep implementing this with each new problem that surfaces in your life, you clear more space within for the light to be felt, and you do it in a shorter length of time with each occurrence. Eventually, all is cleared, the light shines through your being, and you easily see through dilemmas in a day's time. (Caveat: with the big issues in one's life, for example, forgiving others or misplaced drives, you circle around the same pole while gradually ascending on the subject until you fully learn that. Therefore, you retrieve or uncover parts of yourself that you have lost. Life would never leave any part of you behind. You are too precious.

To bring it into your body and feel it there, you first feel the difficulty of your problems and that you are invested in their resolution. Then you search for and implement new solutions, feel the happiness that comes with each resolution, and live a fuller life. With each unloading, you release more tied-up energy, and more light can enter your life. This is felt in your body as a clearer mind, more heartfelt living, and a more stable foundation to live from. The key is sincerely implementing the change in your life. Then, the new energy sequence is worked into your physicality and raises your receptive capacity to your true nature. Your body shifts to more positivity with each implementation of a resolution.

After many such resolutions, you find enough light surges through you to see your true nature is beyond your problems. Once you have seen that there really is no problem, you still need to wrestle with accepting and living your true nature.

This needs to be walked sincerely, just like all the steps that lead up to it. This is on a grand scale because it requires all of your present knowing to walk into the unknowing of your true nature.

Gradually, more and more light and positivity enter your body and life. Little by little it uncovers your true nature. You are more glorious than you can imagine.

THE IMPLICATIONS OF AWAKENING

Access to awakened being, our true nature, is necessary. The route is strewn with past programming, concepts, feelings, and images we have adopted as our lives have proceeded, taking us away from our subtler, more sensitive, and engaged in life layers.

Healing and becoming aware are practices for uncovering and accessing these subtleties of our being. There are multiple ways to do this. A strong intention is needed because the way is difficult but not impossible.

I used the path of knowledge and inquiry for 30 years. This is a left-brain analytical approach. My means utilized Gestalt, Advaita Vedanta and the personal growth of posing a question and applying a new solution. Over the last few years, I have gradually gone over to the path of devotion. Now I solely use that. It is entirely right-brained. Depending on your vehicle's leanings, you will find your way between these two.

I found a powerful access to my true nature through Nisargadatta Maharaj's 'I AM THAT' teachings. This is decidedly a path of devotion. He attained awakening/enlightenment within three years of employing this practice. It did not hit a cord in me years ago when I read his work. I needed to heal/clear away more of my programming before I could hear it, my vehicle's need.

This devotional path has been an intuitive/experiential journey. Somehow, I hit on acknowledging 'I AM' and, with this recognition, a whole new world opened up. A joy wells up with that recognition. Me out of all the universe exists and is present and will never go away. To dwell in that brings me much joy. To stay in that quietly puts me into more peace and joy than I have ever known. I found it to be a gateway.

In this journey, I feel like an infant learning to crawl. All that I have known previously is wiped out, my earthly identity. I now operate by totally different laws, subtle ones. Like, you must stay in the present knowing 'I AM' to stay in this magical life. It belongs to me, but I can't leave myself behind. It's kind of like the feel of putting a faux fur coat on that keeps you warm in below-freezing temperatures, and the moment you take it off, you are back in the cold.

Then there is interacting with others, which has been my life challenge, relationships. I found that I easily popped out of my true nature when I was around others. Then I stepped back and took note, making a point to remain in the 'I AM' state and being true to myself. When I did pop out I noticed I acted like my old same egoic self, not listening as well and directing attention to myself. So, after repeated displays of this, I calmed down, disciplined myself to be true to what I know, and more frequently could maintain my presence and integrity.

Learning to stay in your true nature is a process and becomes stronger the more you do it, thank goodness. Each person has their areas where they will be pulled out, your egoic buttons get pushed. These areas vary from person to person.

The implications of living your true nature are immense. I dare say, my daily life has been revamped. Like impressions come and plans go out the window. I had been impressed, on a deep, subtle level, to attend a Poetry Workshop. The day before, I was talking myself out of it. Then, the strong impression was reimposed. I attended yesterday and was not only able to serve others but was given many suggestions for publishing, which I had been clueless about before. Also, new loves develop and lead you along. I kept feeling drawn to hiking and have been boning up at the gym for my endurance, so I took a wide stab at hiking on an island nearby. It was absolutely delightful. My son and I enjoyed our time together; the scenery was stunning, even though it was a desert-type island, and I collected dead plant sprigs for my painting. I've just decided I need to loosen up about my time.

Your true nature is engaged, and you never know where it will take you. Every day, your senses are heightened, and you are smack dab in the middle of your enlivened life. Connections to everything are stronger. A vastness is felt that lets you breathe clearly at any moment. Everything slows down and is peaceful but, at the same time, alive.

Jesus Christ said, **The Kingdom of Heaven is spread upon the Earth, but men do not see it.**

My journey has not ended. I learn more of my true nature and my engagement in life every day. Believe it or not, you are doing it perfectly for your path.

VULNERABILITY IN POWER

Many things in living our true nature, most natural self, are contradictory, paradoxical. Being in your true nature, using your greatest capital, is a powerful position. Yet, it is so vulnerable that you feel the pulse of the moment and those around you.

Personal power to me is being all I can be and seeing everything and everyone as they are. To achieve this personal power, I need to shed all that is not real inside of me so I can be in touch not only with myself but also with life outside of myself. I must be the pulse that runs through life, my true nature.

There are two basic paths to accomplish this: the path of knowledge and the path of devotion. Practices and disciplines fall into these categories. In Western circles, they are left-brain analytical and right-brain faith/intuition. The path of knowledge is found in Western culture by inquiring, trying out, and then applying to see the results—more the scientific path, if you will. The path of devotion in Western culture is characterized by mainstream religious devotional practice and dependence on a higher power.

In my case, I took the path of knowledge through the Western practices of psychotherapy, Gestalt, and hypnotherapy for decades. These paths revealed to me where my misconceptions were so that I could be more of my true self. Interspersed were glimpses of the joy and freedom of my true nature, which motivated me to continue. Then it turned into a path of devotion, as I saw my reasoning evidence-based learning would take me no further. It is now all devotional in meditating and living the 'I AM,' as taught by Nisargadatta. This is my path, but there are about as many paths as there are people on this Earth. To illustrate, my late husband could not analyze or sort out his foibles, unpack them, and apply new realizations. He would have these moments of clear insight and turn his life around to them, for example, that there is a higher power. Through my years of being on the path of knowledge, he could not relate at all. Obviously, we could not discuss how we came to what we realized. We did discuss new aspects of ourselves that were unlocked, aspects of ourselves that we had gotten in touch with.

The single most difficult thing for me along my path is that I became more vulnerable with each new opening within myself. Vulnerable inside myself to both me and the positive aspects of my environment, for example, nature, love, and beauty. You would think this would be welcome, but my old programming told me that this was not a safe place to be, being more vulnerable. So, it took a bit of time, reassurance, and downtime to get used to each new step. This gradually transitions to being confident in my true nature and the wonder it is, to the point of perceiving everything through it. I found I needed more downtime and quiet time, even amongst others, to get used to this. For a time, I found myself being pulled out of my vulnerable, sensitive state into my old ways of interacting. It took observing this many times over until I could familiarize myself with this old way, accept it, and put my new way into practice.

Putting any new realizations into practice in your daily life is not a straight shot; it twists and turns as you proceed up the mountain. It takes stalwart commitment in the face of what seems like setbacks but is merely steps forward.

The curious thing is that you become more vulnerable as you gain more personal power, evidenced by more freedom, peace, and happiness. Certainly, Christ is seen as a powerful spiritual figure. He could tell when a woman worshiping him touched the hem of his garment. He wept when children sat on his lap at their innocence and preciousness.

When living in my true nature, I am touched by others' kindness towards me in any way. Instead of your buttons getting pushed with feelings of inadequacy, it is replaced with the slightest thing touching your heart. Yet, you see and speak truth regularly and act in a powerful way with integrity in both your personal and global life.

Your true nature is grounded in everyday life, but all the good parts and seeing the less fortunate parts for what they are yet serving where moved upon. It is a mountain to climb, and with each step, the atmospheric conditions change. Then, you find yourself back in everyday life with those same atmospheric conditions you found at the top of the mountain. It's a grand journey and one I am continually grateful for and for each one of you reading this.

SIMPLICITY

I listened
And wandered Finding a
Promising entrance

Stepping in
The entryway
I felt a
Glow

It quickened
All within
Me
And extended out

But to
Remain
Felt like
An ember

I did
Remain
Settling in
Looking about

I became
Accustomed
To the light
Then proceeded

A magic
Enveloped me
Was
Everywhere

All the
Walls of
This dwelling
Fell away

I and
The magic
That is I
Remained

The seeing
Is farseeing
In the multiplicity
Sacredness

No describing
Each Fragment
Seen in its
Nakedness

Beautifully exposed

Relished
Adored
In its simplicity

By Audrey Weigel

THE ETHER OF YOUR BEING

As I journey along in my development I hear and see where certain terms map out my enlightenment experience better and I can understand it more. One spoken by Sadhguru is the Akash, which he defines as ether. The western interpretation is space, which I also find lacking. Ether is the fifth element in eastern religion, beyond the known four elements of earth, water, fire and air.

The ether of your being can only be experienced and not observed. In Western society we want to observe, dissect, test, and draw conclusions with some new property that is discovered. And when this is done, it is often used for deleterious purposes, for example the atomic bomb. I say it is good that we cannot do this to the subtle vital layer of our being, it is reserved for the more refined beings in our world.

During my enlightenment experience, I was a profound awareness, from my deepest core and the ether was my body, I had not bodily sensations, although I had thumped my chest to see if I was dead or not since the shock of being transported to this state was unbelievable to me. I was the ether in my acute awareness, although still distinctly me. I thought to myself, this makes sense since I have always been acutely observant. I looked about and saw the quality of the air about me and through me and it was power and love. It was energetic to the point of power in every inch.

Love pervaded. I had been through many lesser but similar experiences in healing workshops, where you arrive at a foreign overwhelming exhilarating state and are left without words, and I had learned to ask, 'Why are you giving me this?'. So that's what I did. The distinct response spoken to my mind was, 'I have been with you through all your life, minute by minute' and conveyed with overwhelming love and nurturing. This emotionally struck me, and I teared up because I had endured much suffering alone in my life and had to carry on against all odds. I did not see anyone and did not expect this response. The voice spoken to me, my being and the ether were all one. It was not just space but something very energized and so consistent and powerful that I would say it was the body of my awareness/consciousness, even while inhabiting my physical body.

So, what do you do with that knowledge when walking through life, living a life? In my book, 'Altered Perception to Full Awareness, My Personal Journey', I describe my first ten years, after this experience, and how I integrated it into my life. It was a meditative phase of assimilating and yet still doing my life. Some individuals can immediately stay in this real subtle awareness, for example Eckart Tolle. Most cannot and need to assimilate it into their life over time. This was my case.

The ether is an element of our being just like earth, water, fire and air. It is subtle and is the basis of every part of what is. It is more basic and pervasive than what is commonly known. Being enlightened puts you smack dab in the middle of this. Why would a person want to do this? I can hear you, what's the benefit? For earthly life, there is no benefit. You are thrust into another reality that includes this Earth life but on a more subtle aware level. You cannot combine the two, but you can live this new more subtle level while in your regular life.

Living a fuller and then a fuller life by working through negative energies, both within and without, is the key. I postulate that each individual is uniquely composed to resonate to different methods to work through these negative energies.

Let's look at four approaches, methodologies for spiritual unfolding, through the eyes of yogic practices, the four basic types of yoga.

GANA YOGA is the path of knowledge. Being able to discriminate the truth.

RAJA YOGA is the path of calming the mind through meditation

BHAKTI YOGA is the path of devotion

KARMA YOGA is the path of service

The western counterparts are psychotherapy, hypnosis, body work, religion, humanitarian service, astrology, healing work and now meditation as well.

Each person has a different temperament and leanings as to how they operate and by what means they hear, understand and incorporate. These need to be respected. What works for you does not work for me, for example, I could never relate to straight devotion but many the world over absolutely relate to this.

What are we aiming for overall? Being happy, fulfilled and satisfied sounds good to me. When you are aware of and living in the ether, you are deeply satisfied. There is no thinking about it, it pervades your being because it is you and you intimately relate to all about you, seen and unseen.

THE MOTIONLESS MOTION

The still point of our being. Like the Earth in the universe. It appears still to us, yet it is hurtling through space. In like manner, our true nature appears motionless but is connected to a vast field. In Eastern religions, some consider 'ether' to be the fifth element. It is the experiential stratosphere that we belong to, and it is the foundation of our being. You could go so far as to say that it is our body in another dimension.

These are bold claims that go beyond the common scientifically accepted data. In fact, they cannot be known within the present scientific framework. They can only be known through one's experience in these more subtle realms.

As we proceed through the various stages of life, from childhood to adulthood, we do have experiences, but they are limited to this physical realm, of which mind and body are an integral part. Occasionally, the subtle realm presents itself; for example, when we have an acute experience of self, reduced to our most basic self, where we are hyper-focused on joy or sorrow, everything else falls away—for example, the birth of a child or the death of a loved one. Let's take being hyper-focused, as in a performance in sports or the arts, when there is only the moment and our presence, and it just slowly flows. Or perhaps it comes unbidden in a totally encompassing experience, such as an enlightenment experience.

As a seeker, these moments come. We might then feel there must be more to this life than we currently know. This is motivation enough to proceed in our spiritually progressive journey or at least to question our beliefs and way of doing things.

In fact, there is much more than what we think about and perceive with our senses, but that does us no good if we do not know it. Being open to the possibility of there being more is key. There is a need to explore and confirm not only with our thinking and sensing but also through our experiences.

In my life experiences, past the three-quarters of a century mark at this point, I have not put stock in anything unless I have experienced it. A time when I took a left turn instead of a right turn was 14 years ago when I had an enlightenment experience. It was a more real and authentic experience of my core of being and what I was a part of than anything I had experienced in my regular life. Over the following 10 years, I explored and grew into embodying that. Through these subtle and sometimes not-so-subtle experiences, I learned that there is more to life than what we can think and perceive with our senses.

It's not been an easy ascent up the mountain, or it could be described as a descent into the center of my being. This was getting in touch with and living my authentic, true nature, living in the light. My journey from Western healing modalities to Eastern practices was instrumental in this. Now, I employ the practice of bhakti yoga, which is devotion. In Western terms, it is devotion to your God or your higher power.

In living in the light, it is not a done deal. There are still triggers within me, and circumstances without that intrude. For instance, I went to a high-end arts festival in a resort town near where I live this weekend. My son and I sat down at a table next to the line of booths for a snack. I found myself looking at people more than the art. I noticed their clothing and relationships as they walked by. I found the experience unsatisfying at a deep level and thought, 'This is no fun; I should have stayed home.' Then, I also noticed that I viewed them superficially and not in their soul essence; I realized I was letting the circumstances keep me out of my being, being in my head and not immersed in my true being, the present experience. I stopped and meditated for a bit, to myself while sitting with my eyes open, and got in touch with my true essence deep inside me. Upon doing that, the whole scenario changed for me. I started focusing on my son eating this fanciful appetizer and conversing with him about what we liked and didn't like. Then, we proceeded to go along the row of booths. I could engage in what struck my interest. Also, I had no qualms about having authentic conversations with artists. One artist was doing a demo; I joked with him that his painting was in the ugly teenage phase. I knew this because I painted myself. This stage in a painting is when you first put in the structure and the background's general colors, and it just looks plain. I told him I paint, sew, and write myself. He asked what I wrote about. Then we proceeded to have a lively, illuminating discussion on both our parts. He asked about a personal reflective moral dilemma. Then a past customer of his came up and I told him I would email him. I thought I could throw some ideas his way that would be applicable in his Christian belief system. I share this to illustrate that there is a night and day difference to living when you live in your true being vs your mind. I stopped being in my head and came into the immediate experience. Living in your mind is factual, analytical, and not engaging or fascinating. When you live from your ineffable true nature, it is juicy and of the utmost interest because you are present/aware, and there is a quality of aliveness that cannot be lived but by any other means.

Note that I came around to recognizing that the circumstances were triggering me, and then I returned to my true nature. This getting triggered is natural since there were 60 years of familial and society conditioning, where I ran on automatic, that I need to be able to recognize and see through. I suggest being patient with the process and knowing that it is a matter of returning to your innocence and purity, which will happen the more you feel this place that feels like home within you.

I have heard that in some Buddhist monasteries, they used to call monks that have come in to live in the light, their true nature, baby Buddhas. It's a whole new stratosphere to live in; it operates by different properties, and your life focus is completely different. You could call it unfocused, as to worldly goals and projects, with peace and satisfaction within the moment being sufficient unto itself as you experience it.

I hesitate to talk too much about the attributes of living in the light, fearing you will conceptualize it and aim for that. Rupert Spira said, "You cannot know yourself; you can only be yourself." There is no conceptualizing it. You allow yourself to be and let whatever comes come and whatever goes go, this occurs naturally.

TO MY GRANDSON

Yesterday when we played pickleball together, you barely beat me. You mentioned that you like getting books that your Dad recommends. However, he gave you a book that you truly do not understand, the 'Tao Te Ching'. I could understand why you could not comprehend it, he is 15 years old today. I am going to a birthday dinner at a steakhouse with the family later today. He also has a twin brother that is into football, as he is but he has an academic side to him too. I told him the history of how Lao Tze wrote the 'Tao Te Ching', as I heard it. That he was a realized sage and went about teaching China, in the 6th century, but no one wanted to hear. He finally became so averse to teaching that he went off by himself. On his way out, he was asked to write down his knowledge and that is the 'Tao Te Ching'. That the various ideograms, 64 of them, are the changes or energies that we all go through in life. I told my grandson that there are more interpretive versions, easier to understand, that break each ideogram down into dysfunctional, functional and gifted. He said, "Gifted?". I said yes, when you get the energy or lesson of the ideogram to a masterful stage. After we were done with the games, I said we could stop by my home and get the more easily understood version of the 'Tao Te Ching' and go to ice cream and look it over. At first he agreed and then when I asked him again, wanting to make sure this was his desire, he said he would rather go straight home. I said I will bring it over sometime. It is 'Gene Keys' by Richard Rudd. I studied this for many years. It gives a practical way to understand and practice spirituality and being your true self.

This goes along with an inspiration I was given during one of my studies, "There is only cycles of knowing", I was told through spirit. This rang true to me. I saw that I have not been able to hold on to my past, that it is more like a dream, calling into question its validity. All I am is what I know now for sure. Relating this to the 'TAO TE CHING', I thought that it is only what I know that puts me in touch with the life that goes along with it, what is real to me at the time, and this is a cycle because there is always another cycle of knowing that will come.

The only thing I know is that 'I am', that present knowledge of being aware. I know that I am for sure. Not by any deductive scientific reasoning, but in my experience, I know I am. This is fundamental and necessary knowledge and must be authentically recognized and accepted in order to awaken. This is difficult and brings up fears because it is like walking off a bridge, you don't know what is on the other side but you know you will never be the same. Once you cross you are your true self which is foreign to your present idea of yourself. It is a wonderful state of being but it takes a hell of a lot of courage to walk off that bridge or you have to trust someone, a teacher, so much that you do it. Sometimes you go back and forth until you are convinced that it is the only way and the truth and then you jump off and stay there.

In western terms, Maslow and Jung both saw self-realization as the end goal of their philosophies and goals. Awakening also includes becoming a part of something much greater than yourself. You could say that the experience of being awake takes away your history/past identity and makes you an all-present potential which is part life and others. You become a wide expanse but nevertheless you are still awake and aware.

Sadguru told a lovely story in a podcast recently, about 4 yogi's and how the universe saved them from a violent storm, metaphor for life as we know it. They would each argue that their own type of yoga was the solution to achieving enlightenment. The four yoga's are, Jnana through intellect/deduction, Kriya through energy, Karma through action/service and Bhakti through devotion/love. The storm put them in such a position that they had to come together, and the universe ended the storm due to all of them finally getting together. All these aspects are needed to live in your true self and be embedded in that.

I think the story of the 4 yogis' coming together is an apt description of my path. For me it has been mostly using intellectual deduction through various therapies, the last ten years Eastern methods of self-study/application and then this last year devotion to truth as it presents itself. Serving others with my love and knowledge when indicated, as well.

If none of your efforts have produced any results, then I would question your intent. Intent is the key before anything else. By results I mean that you are happier and more content with yourself, even though you see more you would like to have answered. With most people and myself included, it is the little steps that count and add up to big results.

You have to be determined that when you are asked to give up something for truth then you do, no matter what it is and how long it will take. Because you will be asked to give up all of what is known to you, your delusions that do not seem like it at the time and walk into a new true reality. Hence, Adyashanti's book, titled 'The End of Your World'. Commitment to truth is necessary. And what do you get for all this giving up? You get yourself and the truth about yourself and the gift of a present aware life encounter. The end of suffering as you know it. If you have a service to perform then it will well up in you and you will proceed with satisfaction that you are a small part of what is happening but nevertheless you made a difference.

PASSION

If I were to tell you that your true nature, connected to your higher power, wants you passionate and engaged in your life, would you believe it? What an odd idea, consumed with a drive that is aligned with your passions. Your passions, not anyone else's. Seems foreign to the modern boring or distracted way of life.

I propose that our limiting ideas and concepts damper down, if not irradicate, our enthusiasm and engagement in this life. What if we just operated on our passions? Sure, we have obligations but if we have a modicum of free time and energy then let's go off the deep end and take a dive. That could be a good start.

The last few days all I have been doing is following my passions. For me, that is oil painting landscapes and studying 'how to' podcasts. Thrown in there is going to the gym and visiting with loved ones. One morning I woke at 5am and thought, why not get up now and start painting. That I did and it brought considerable happiness down deep inside me. Last evening, I left a football game at half time because I was bored. I kept looking at the surrounding hills and figuring out what colors I would mix if I were painting it.

Of late, my practice has been, the way of energy through getting in touch with my true nature and remaining there. This involves taking a minute at my morning studies and going deeply into my being (described in a poem at the end of this article) and committing to remain there throughout my day. At first, during my day, I would be thrown out of just being. Then I recognized who or what was throwing me off. As time went on, I could more easily spot these things as they came up, for example, going into completely 'other focused mode' vs remaining present in my being, listening and responding from there. As time progressed, the territory became known to me, and I could navigate it.

I am guessing that my mentioning my practice of late is about as meaningful to you as saying that I hit my head with the dull side of an axe. Why do I mention that? Everyone has their practice that works best for them. So, when I mention mine, you probably cannot relate. As a reference, I now mention four types of yoga and how they facilitate getting to your true nature.

1. Jnani, the way of knowledge
2. Kriya, the way of energy
3. Karma, the way of service
4. Bhakti, the way of devotion

These were all mentioned in a podcast by Sadguru, a Hindu guru from southern India where he has the Isha Institution.

Previously, I had employed all but the way of energy. Mind you, I rarely do yoga but practice these using Western methods, for example, the way of knowledge through healing work. I suggest settling on one of these, to begin with. As my needs changed, I have used all four at different times in my practice.

These practices can shed light on what concepts and beliefs are outdated in your belief system. We are often put in positions where it benefits us to move forward as opposed to staying in the same mode with consequences. They can give you permission to evolve and go on to what is true for you, thereby bringing more happiness to your life. I have seen the need to be an adventurer because the new territory can seem foreign. After all, we haven't been privileged to that much fun and excitement since we were children.

Until you come to the part where you give yourself all the permission to engage your passions while being fully present. Yes, it feels like you're crazed but in a good way, excited about life and what you are engaged in. Your greatest gift to yourself and the world is you being authentically in your true nature. Dr. Seuss is applicable here, "Today you are You, that is *truer than true*. There is no one alive who is Youer than You."

HERE

Present
The elevator goes down
Until it hits
Bottom floor

Past
Thinking
Feeling
Wants

Bottom floor
Where
There seems
To be nothing

But it's
Comfortable
And unexpectedly
Light

There's
A seeing
And acceptance
Here

BEING

This month has been revelatory for me. I experienced a number of difficult circumstances. From a major drug raid next door—I woke up to an armored vehicle in front of their home—to the other neighbor attempting to manipulate me so I would not report their blaring music. Then having my love interest go in another direction. Plus visiting my long-lost sister for a week and finding I could not relate to her except in exchanging our love for each other, due to her negativity. Maintaining my being through it all yet disheartened at the occurrences.

I found that I did not leave room for negative behaviors and unexpected turns of events, which was surprising to me.

Listening to a podcast by Swami Sarvapriyananda on the book Ashtavakra, he spoke on the impermanence of all we experience. For example, people come and go, circumstances come and go, our bodies come and go, and our feelings come and go. However, the awareness that is me is always present through it all. To be anchored in our being is our stability. We are present throughout. We treasure that.

Things come and things go, yet we remain. To see the passing of relationships, possessions, and circumstances, yet anchor in our true being. And relate to what speaks to us in that moment of our lives. We all exist at different levels of knowing the truth of our being.

Circumstances and relationships have little sway on us when we can view from a solid anchored point. Like a lighthouse watching the ships go in and out of the harbor. Yes, we are compassionate when a ship comes in damaged or sinks while at sea but we remain to interact with and guide others. We are anchored in our firm awareness as the 'I AM' and function from there because it is our true being.

BEING

What I am doing
Does not work
I am banging
My head against
A wall

I have
Tried
Everything
I know

I now
GIVE UP
Trying
For I am spent

I request
New insights
To push me
Closer to my being
My happiness

A NEW WAY OF BEING

Why would one want a new way of being? Is the present way of being unsatisfactory in some way? Where did that dissatisfaction come from? These are things to be explored. Each one of us is the author of our own creation. A friend of mine said, "If I have a problem then all I have to do is look in the mirror".

We all learn in different ways. To be simplistic, like visual and auditory learners take input in through different channels. Learning from life can be done through paths of finding knowledge, learning from actions taken, energy work or devotion to a higher power. These are paths that are taken in both Western and Eastern cultures. For example, my close friend had a mind-bending revelation that there is a God, while driving at age 50. He turned to religion and practiced from that point onward. I have taken each one of those life learning modes for extended periods of time on my path. It can be a singularly dedicated path or utilize various practices, all according to the way the individual hears and sees. I find this understanding of different learning modes helpful when I am scratching my head at others relating how an experience taught them something, for example, when I am in a knowledge-based learning mode and they learned through devotion to a higher power.

Resolution of our conflicts and questions is key to our progress toward our happiness and peace. It is through the above-mentioned paths that this can be achieved. For example, I am currently walking a path of energy. I meditate and stay in that energy during that day. Bear with me while I site an example in my personal life. This week I became frustrated at not being able to produce the results I wanted in a painting class I am taking. Through talking with friends, I saw that I need to be more patient, that translates into studying the course material more thoroughly and applying that. My excuse is that I am more of a quick study, get to the bottom line, implement it type of person. Unbeknownst to me, being more patient has helped me in my meditative practice as well. I would like to point out that there are many ways to get your conflicts resolved and questions answered. Some direct and some open to the flow of internal and external happenings, such as my personal example.

We are all striving for happiness and peace. We have preconceived ideas of how to get there and what it is like when we arrive. What if happiness and peace were found through different means and looked different when we arrived? Your spiritual path is a means to unravel this puzzle. This leads to your 'true self', which is where this unexpected happiness and peace resides.

With each new realization, a bit of knowledge, realized through whatever means, speaks to you, you will be faced with a new way of being. This will feel foreign at first but ring true. Press on with incorporating and after a while it will seem natural. A new surge of energy will be experienced, for you have released some locked-up energy that you have been limping along with.

ON THE SUBJECT OF ENLIGHTENMENT

Trust that life knows better than you do. To use an old saying, 'The proof is in the pudding'. In other words, the results speak for themselves. Are you happier and more peaceful with this new way of life, in little or big ways?

The final stretch before living in the light full time, awakening or enlightenment, is to recognize that this true self IS the true you. That all you have thought before was you is dross in the wind, means nothing except it was the means to this end. You come to the knowledge that the words I AM, or I AM THAT I KNOW I AM carry the fast track to your sacred being. Or through meditation you have found this place deep inside your being and you practice staying there. Or you have an enlightenment experience and experience this straight up. The way you travel to the core of your being is not important. What is important is that you recognize your true self, your essence, and see it as the truth or that you come to find that it is the truth over time.

After there is recognition of your true self, then accepting it comes. It is not a head trip but a deep personal awakening. One lives in an entirely different realm that includes this temporary 3D world but from an authentic seeing. One possesses purity, so much so that there are no limits or edges to the true self. One's energy has no limits, and you sincerely are one with everyone, able to tap into their essence and enjoy their presence. You, your energy self, extends in all directions and is vast and unlimited. This takes a while to assimilate. Adyashanti said, in his book THE END OF YOUR WORLD, that in olden days inside monasteries they used to think of the newly awakened as baby Buddhas.

When the dust settles down, getting familiar with your true being and living from there, one is so centered and peaceful that there is no motivation to seek or particularly to do. It is calm and a fulfillment in itself. The best gift you could imagine. Being returned to yourself, in full bloom. You are fully you and connected to authenticity in your engagement in the world. Your individual fulfillment is what wells up inside you minute to minute, being in the flow of your being. It is flexible and you can be highly focused in the moment when called for. Your compassion and how it manifests might direct you to serve. Perhaps to quietly live out your days in that awakened state, as Ramana Maharshi did.

www.ingramcontent.com/pod-product-compliance
Lightning Source LLC
LaVergne TN
LVHW041631070426
835507LV00008B/562